Psychology 101

How To Control, Influence, Manipulate and Persuade Anyone

Anthony Kane

Copyright 2015 by Anthony Kane.

Published by Make Profits Easy LLC

Profitsdaily123@aol.com

facebook.com/MakeProfitsEasy

Table of Contents

Introduction 5
Chapter 1: Social Influence 7
   Sources of Social Influence 9
   Cialdini's Principles of Social Influence 10
   Kelman's varieties of social influence 13
Chapter 2: Minority Influence 17
   Factors that play a role in minority influence 18
Chapter 3: Reactance 22
Chapter 4: Obedience 26
   Studies in Obedience 27
Chapter 5: Persuasion 34
   Attribution Theory 39
   Conditioning Theories 40
   Cognitive Dissonance Theory 42
   Social Judgement Theory 43
   Inoculation theory 45
   Narrative transportation theory 45
   Methods of Persuasion 46
Chapter 6: Social Impact Theory 54
Chapter 7: Reverse Psychology 59
Chapter 8: Practical Application of Social Influence 61

In Business 61
During presentations 65
In Social Settings and Everyday Life 71
In Relationships 81
Conclusion 89

Introduction

Throughout history, we have witnessed mankind being moved to action such as engaging in war, racism, religious intolerance, and ethnic cleansing. These are all products of persuasion, where people were presented with information beforehand and were then convinced that they needed to engage in actions regardless of how terrifying in order to act on their beliefs.

Today, in a smaller and less harmful scale, we are still exposed to many kinds of persuasion even if we aren't fully aware of it. We encounter hundreds of ads on a daily basis through televisions, computers, radio, and even the people we meet may try to convince us of something.

The topic of persuasion is one of the most interesting matters in psychology today. In short it is described as the ability to convince a person or group of people to change their beliefs strong enough to act on them. Persuasion can come in many forms and its success also depends on many other factors.

In this book you will learn about the many aspects involved with persuasion.

Readers will learn:

- The different kinds of social influence: compliance, conformity, and internalization
- The definition of conformity
- Famous studies conducted as an attempt to explain obedience
- Principles of social influence
- How to be a good persuader in various situations: in business, social settings, and in relationships

Chapter 1: Social Influence

Social influence is a major branch in psychology that examines how a person's actions, thoughts, and beliefs are influenced by social groups. When a person succeeds in changing a person's beliefs or actions, this results in conformity.

According to Harold Gerard and Morton Deutsch, there are two psychological needs that lead individuals to conform to expectations of other people. These are:

1. Informational social influence: Addresses one's need to be right. Informational social influence happens more likely when people are uncertain thereby are willing to accept information from other people as evidence.

2. Normative social influence: Addresses one's need to be liked by others. Normative social influence arises out of one's need to conform to other peoples' positive expectations. According to Kelman, normative influence results in public

compliance as compared to informational social influence which results in private acceptance.

These are the factors that affect conformity:

1. Difficulty: When a task is seen as difficult, this can lead to decreased or increased conformity. When a person doesn't know how to perform a task they are more likely to conform although when it is perceived as more difficult people are usually more accepting of different responses that result in conformity.

2. Individual differences: Decreased tendency to conform is linked in people who have motivation to achieve and have stronger leadership characteristics.

3. Group size: Conformity is more likely to happen in groups of 3 to 5 people.

4. Situational character: Individuals are more likely to conform if the situation is ambiguous and they are not sure how to respond best.

5. Cultural differences: People coming from collectivist cultures are more likely to conform than others.

Sources of Social Influence

On broad terms, there are 3 sources of social influences currently recognized by psychologists. In short, people are influenced through these 3 sources:

1. Social Institutions: These include political parties, labor unions, and organized religion.

2. Interactions with other people: The types of people we interact with at work, at home, and at social settings are sources of social influence.

3. Individual socialization: Refers to the amount of socialization an individual receives and is open to. Socialization is a process that inducts humans to a culture or society, and begins as early as infancy. Products of socialization include the language we speak, the ideas and beliefs we hold to be true, and our own characteristics and behavior.

Cialdini's Principles of Social Influence

The 6 principles of social influence are in a nutshell, described as how an individual can influence others to say yes. These were created by renowned psychologist Robert Cialdini as published in his 1984 book, "Influence: The Psychology of Persuasion".

1. Reciprocity: It is part of human nature to return favors and generally treat others as we are treated. The principle of reciprocity states that humans feel obliged offer favors and discounts to other people if they were offered to us as well. This behavior arises because humans generally feel uncomfortable when they are faced with feeling indebted to other people.

For example, if a supplier offers you a large discount for purchasing from them in bulk you may be prompted to buy more from them. If a coworker helps you during a busy project, you may feel obliged to buy them lunch to return the favor, or support their ideas in the long run.

2. Commitment and Consistency: According to Cialdini, humans have an innate desire for consistency. This is why when we commit to something we are more encouraged to follow through until the end.

For example, if you show interest in a coworker's idea when they first discussed this with you, you would be more inclined to support his project proposal.

3. Social Proof: This principle of social influence is also referred to as "safety in numbers". People are more inclined to act when others are doing the same. This includes eating in busier restaurants, or taking on overtime schedules if coworkers are doing the same. Individuals are more vulnerable to this principle of social influence when they are feeling uncertain or if the people are similar to us.

4. Liking: People are more easily influenced by those that they like. A person's likability may come in various forms, such as their familiarity or similarity to us, when they give us

compliments, or simply the fact that we trust them more than others. People are more likely to buy from people that they already know and trust. For this reason, companies that utilize the services of sales agents employ them from existing communities so that more people are familiar with them and end up buying.

5. Authority: People naturally feel obliged to people who are viewed with a sense of authority. This is the reason why advertising companies often hire authorities in certain fields to advertise their products. For example, dentists promoting toothpaste, doctors promoting medication, athletes promoting shoes. It is also because when a person is authoritative over us that we tend to say yes, such as when a manager asks us to complete a task. Certain things can also lend an air of authority, such as the use of uniforms, job titles, and other accessories.

6. Scarcity: According to the scarcity principle of social influence, people are more inclined to like something when it has limited availability.

People are more likely to purchase something when they are told that it is the last of its kind available, or it is offered at a discount that will expire soon.

Oftentimes, these 6 principles are used to mislead people such as by getting them to purchase products at high prices. Using this approach is always best when you are convincing people to do something that is good for them. It is always best to be honest, such as providing factual information for people to make a well-informed decision.

Kelman's varieties of social influence

When people change their opinion as a result of persuasion or social influence, this results in 3 types of changes:

1. **Compliance:** Occurs when a person seems to agree with a request and will act on it to please others. Even if they do not agree with the opinion they will keep their personal beliefs private. Compliance usually happens with simple acts when individuals do not feel it is necessary

to question the request or because they are not being asked to invest emotionally. An example of compliance is when office rules require being silent at all times, or passing the salt at the dinner table.

As a general rule, people comply when they feel that they should because by challenging the request the consequences would be greater and more uncomfortable. People at work obey rules because they know that by going against it, suspension and possible dismissal are bigger consequences as compared to simply following the rules. Compliance also largely deals with the concepts of pain and pleasure, and people comply mostly because they are after a reward such as general approval.

2. Identification: Occurs when individuals identify with the person from whom the idea originated. In this variety of social influence, a person will believe an argument and will not question it. Identification is attributed to several factors. First, it may happen when the speaker is a recognized social leader and we desire to be associated with them by accepting their statements even if there is compliance here to some degree. When we identify ourselves with a group this means that we accept their values and rules, a characteristic that is also observed in a group of friends. Second, identification also happens when we accept someone's teachings and accept all that they say. Third and last, identification can happen when a person wants to be like the other person. This is common behavior among fans of musicians or actors, and is also a result of brainwashing.

3. Internalization: Occurs when an individual fully accepts and adopts an idea or a belief proposed by another. It is a more personal kind of opinion change wherein a person does so without coercion from others and without the need to associate or be liked by others. It requires more cognitive processing because before we fully adopt an idea, we think about it more deeply and see how it fits into our existing beliefs and values. Internalized ideas need to make sense to the listener and the argument used by the persuader is often rational. In other situations, internalization may occur because the persuader is passionate about the idea which stimulates the emotions of the listener resulting in a change of opinion.

Chapter 2: Minority Influence

Minority influence occurs when the majority accepts the beliefs of a minority. It is usually successful only after a long period of time and results in private acceptance of the minority's views. According to Moscovici, majority influence is based on public compliance, most likely due to normative social influence. Because of this, the power of numbers plays a significant role. The majority will have the power to approve and disapprove resulting in added pressure on minorities to conform.

Majority groups are not concerned about the opinions of minorities regarding them, this is why minority influence isn't based on normative persuasion. Minority influence is based largely on informational persuasion such as when they are able to provide the majority with new sources and kinds of information they were not exposed to before, causing them to re-evaluate their own views and opinions. Because of this, minority influence results in internalization by convincing them that the views of the minority are correct.

Factors that play a role in minority influence

1. Behavioral Style: This is made up of 4 components: consistency, confidence of the minority in the views they present, absence of bias, and the resistance of social pressure. According to Moscovici, consistency is the most important behavioral style. When a minority is unchanging and consistent in their views, the majority is more likely to be persuaded. Moscovici undertook several studies to prove this point, further adding that consistency is important because:

- Consistency shows the majority that the minority is committed to their views and they are convinced they are right.
- When the majority is faced with a consistent opposition they are more likely to rethink their beliefs.

- When the majority is confronted with a minority who's confident and dedicated to their viewpoint, they are more likely to think that the opposing group has a point.
- Consistent minorities may create conflict and uncertainty by disrupting accepted norms. When this happens the majority usually takes the minority view more seriously. This results in the majority group questioning their own beliefs.

2. Style of Thinking: If you think deeply about the views expressed by the minority, you are engaging in systematic thinking. On the other hand, if you simply dismiss the minority's views without thinking about it in much detail you are engaging in superficial thinking. When a minority can persuade the majority to invest time thinking about issues as well as any arguments for or against it then they are more likely to influence the majority. In other words, if the minority is able to encourage discussions about an argument that they are pushing for they are likely to influence the majority.

3. Flexibility and compromise: Another important factor in determining minority influence is how the majority views the consistency of the minority. In the event that the minority is viewed as being rigid, inflexible, and uncompromising, it is less likely that the majority will change their opinions. However if they are seen as open to compromise and flexible they are perceived as less extreme and therefore will be more successful in influencing the majority.

4. Identification: It is human nature for individuals to identify with people who they perceive as similar to them. Women tend to identify with other women, Europeans with other Europeans, and so on. Psychology studies state that when the majority is able to identify themselves with the minority then it is more likely for them to take the views of the minority seriously and change their existing beliefs.

Minority influence isn't only observed in social groups. It is also largely present in the workplace. When an organization integrates minority influence, it can encourage diversity as well as positive change.

Chapter 3: Reactance

As humans, we have an innate need for freedom which is particularly activated when we feel that there is a restriction placed on our opinions or actions. The natural tendency is for people to react with resistance when we are faced with a restrictive force. In essence, the response is fighting back any limiting influences. According to Brehm, psychological reactance is a force that arises when a person fights for their own freedom. It is also aroused when an individual is given an order or told that a certain activity is prohibited. When people are told that they cannot have something, the more they will want it.

Reactance can occur when individuals are under pressure to accept an attitude or view. As a result they may end up adopting a view that is contrary to the intended influence, also leading to a resistance in persuasion. To prevent this, some people utilize reverse psychology to successfully persuade a person. We'll discuss reverse psychology a little more later on.

The 4 elements of reactance theory include:

- Perceived freedom
- Threat to freedom
- Reactance
- Restoration of freedom

Reactance theory also assumes that individuals perceive there are free behaviors that they can choose to engage in at any given time. Free behavior can refer to any activity that a person can participate in, and they will only see it to be free if they have the psychological and physical abilities to do so. Furthermore, free behavior can refer to any act, ones does or doesn't do, or how one does something. Each time a person has free behavior they are more likely to experience reactance when that particular behavior is restricted or threatened with elimination.

The rules associated with reactance and free behavior:

1. If a free behavior is removed or threatened with elimination, the more important it is to the individual and thus the greater the extent of their reactance. This is because the level of reactance is directly related to the importance of the behavior to the person.

2. Within a set of free behaviors, the greater the amount that is eliminated, the more significant the level of reactance will be.

3. If a free behavior is deemed important and is threatened with elimination, the threat and level of reactance will also be greater.

In individual experiences of reactance, it is not assumed that a person can be aware of the reactance. However in the situation that they are aware of reactance they understand that if they can do what they want they also do not have to do things that they don't want to. If it is solely freedom that is being explored, the person always wants to be responsible for directing their own behavior.

In situations where social pressure threatens freedom, a person may resist that pressure as a form of reactance.

Chapter 4: Obedience

Obedience is a type of social influence where individuals act to respond to a direct order usually coming from a figure of authority. With obedience, we assume that the individual would not have acted in such a way without the presence of the direct order.

Obedience happens when you are told to do something by another person. It is different from conformity which happens through social pressure because it is the norm of the majority. The main difference is that obedience involves hierarchy and a person who has a status of authority. In obedience, the person giving the order always enjoys a higher power from the person who is receiving the order.

Culturally, obedience is perceived as a virtue especially within families. It has always been expected that children obey their elders. Other instances in history that demonstrate obedience are slavery, serfs in feudal societies, patriarchy, and how people behave according to their religion. During conventional Christian weddings, obedience was included as part of the bride's vows together with honor and love. However this was removed when women's suffrage came along as well as the feminist movements. Today, the promise to obey is an optional vow in Christian weddings.

Obeying authority has also been viewed as a basic aspect of human social organizations. Almost every society has created a system of hierarchy where some people exercise authority over others. Basic examples of this include the police having authority over the public, and teachers having authority over their students.

Studies in Obedience
1. The Milgram Experiment: Stanley
Milgram carried out one of the most famous and controversial studies in psychology, known as the Milgram experiment. The experiment was prompted by the acts of genocide that occurred in the holocaust, where the defense statement of

accused individuals participating in crime attributed it to "obedience".

Milgram was interested in understanding the extent that people would go in obeying a figure of authority even if it meant placing harm on another person. He recruited 40 male volunteers for a lab experiment, who were between the ages of 20 and 50. They were paid a fee of $4.50 upon arrival. When the experiment began, participants were introduced to another participant who was an associate of Milgram. Straws were drawn to determine their roles whether they were to play teacher or learner. This act was rigged, as the associate always ended up playing the learner role. Also present was an experimenter who wore a lab coat and was played by an actor.

The experiment was held in 2 rooms of the Yale Interaction Library. One room was reserved for the learner and had an electric chair. Another room was used by the teacher and experimenter with a machine used to generate electric shock on the chair. The learner, played by Mr. Wallace, was strapped to an electric chair. He was made to learn a list of word pairs after which the teacher tested him by naming a word and asking him to recall the word pair from a list of choices. Each time he made a mistake, the teacher administered electric shock whose intensity increased with the number of mistakes made. The learner gave incorrect answers on purpose and each time, the teacher administered electric shock. If the teacher refused to shock the learner, he was given a series of orders to make sure that he continued.

The findings of the Milgram experiment showed that ordinary people will obey orders given by a figure of authority, even if it means harming an innocent human. The obedience to authority is ingrained in us as humans from the way we were raised.

2. The Zimbardo Experiment: Another classic study on obedience conducted in Stanford University in the 1970's, the Zimbardo experiment involved college students who were placed in a mock prison environment so that researchers could investigate the impact of various social forces on the behavior of people in prison situations. Stanford students played the role of prisoners and prison guards, and were paid $15 per day for participation in the experiment.

Participants were randomly assigned to their role, keeping in mind that the prison environment was kept as close to reality as possible. "Prisoners" were arrested at their own homes and without warning, followed by investigation at a local police station. "Guards" were given khaki uniforms to wear alongside basic accessories that included handcuffs, whistles, and dark glasses to prevent the ability to make eye contact with the prisoners. Physical violence was not permitted in this kind of experiment. Zimbardo continued to observe the behavior of both prisoners and guards.

Participants who played the prisoner role were treated just like any other criminal; they were photographed and fingerprinted. Then they were blindfolded and taken to Stanford's psychology department where Zimbardo had the mock prison set up. Upon arrival, prisoners were stripped of their clothing, deloused, had all possessions removed, and were only given prison clothes to wear. They were also given a uniform and were referred to as a number.

Within a short time frame, participants quickly settled into their role of guard and prisoner although it was observed that guards adopted their new roles faster. The guards soon began harassing prisoners, behaving in a sadistic manner and seemed to be enjoying it. The prisoners were insulted and were given a set of boring tasks and were also dehumanized.

Soon, prisoners began displaying prisoner-like behavior. Most of the time they discussed issues in the prison and told on one another to the guards. They also took the prison rules seriously, and some even started siding with the guards against other prisoners who did not obey the rules. Over the course of a few days, the relationship between the prisoners and guards began to change, where a change in a person resulted to a change in another. Guards remained in control and prisoners were dependent on them. The dependency from the prisoners led to a change in attitude from the guards, they became more derisive and grew contempt for the prisoners. Because they were so dependent on the guards, the prisoners kept on finding ways to please them.

Thirty six hours into the experiment, a prisoner had to be released because he was screaming and crying uncontrollably. He began showing symptoms of entering into a deep depression. A few days later, other prisoners followed suit after showing symptoms of emotional disorders despite being pronounced normal just before the experiment. Although Zimbardo intended for the experiment to run for a fortnight, he had to shut it down by day 6. Participants may suffer from physical or mental damage if it continued to go on.

The conclusion from Zimbardo's experiment was that people will readily conform to the social roles they are expected to play. This is particularly true if the roles are strongly stereotyped such as the role of the prison guard. It was also found that having a pseudo prison environment was crucial in investigating obedience and behavior in this case, because none of the participants displayed sadistic tendencies prior to the experiment. This showed that the roles people play are a large part of shaping their attitudes and behavior.

Chapter 5: Persuasion

Persuasion is defined as the process by which a communicator tries to influence other people into changing their behavior or attitude about an issue by transmitting a message. The key elements of persuasion are:

- Persuasion is symbolic where the communicator should be using words, sounds, images, and others.
- Persuasion is a deliberate effort to change a person's beliefs or opinions.
- Self-persuasion is necessary because people should be free to choose.
- The method in which the message is communicated can happen through a variety of means such as verbal and nonverbal, through the radio, internet, or direct communication.

However, not all kinds of communication have the ability to persuade people as it may be meant to entertain or simply to provide information.

The act of persuasion can be used to manipulate people which is why trying to persuade others may be seen as revolting behavior. Persuasion, when analyzed as a process, can be differentiated from communication as a cause of stimulus to the associated behavioral changes that result as the effect or the response.

Here we will look at the steps that a person experiences when they are being persuaded. First there is the presence of communication wherein the receiver will pay attention to the content brought forward. He will then try to comprehend the contents of the communication as a whole, including trying to comprehend what the speaker is trying to say. This includes trying to comprehend the suggested conclusion that is being urged by the speaker as well as any evidence which may be provided to support the conclusion. Persuasion only occurs when the individual eventually accepts or agrees with the point being provided and he should retain this interest long enough for him to act on it. The primary goal of persuasion is for the individual or a group of people to adopt a new attitude. Examples of this including switching a brand of cereal because of new information being presented to them, or when a person changes his religious beliefs.

Some theorists emphasize that there is a difference between educating and persuading. While persuasion and education are similar in the sense that they are both providing new information through communication, they are not always the same. Repetitive communication can influence learning which shows that at some point it has a persuasive impact on individuals. Similarly, there are principles in verbal communication that are also widely used by successful persuaders. One way to look at this is the repeated use of advertisements in television that provide information as a means of attempting to convince the consumer to make an educated change in behavior such as using another brand of toothpaste because they now believe it is healthier for them. The way one reacts to a persuasive message will of course depend on the message itself and the way an individual perceives or interprets it. Persuasion, according to perceptual theorists, is the process by which a person's perception or attitudes are changed. There is also evidence that states that the success of persuasion depends on a person's preconceptions which are equally as important as the message.

In discussing persuasion, it is also important to note that persuasion also deals with finding a compromise among conflicting forces, according to some theorists. These forces include existing attitudes and biases, a person's individual desires, social pressures, and new information. This conflict resolution model is also referred to as balance, congruity, or consistency. It deals with how people compromise their existing forces and realign it with their existing attitudes. According to some theorists, persuasion deals with an intellectual aspect while for others it deals with the emotional considerations.

The 4 major ways in which persuasion differs today from how it was in the past:

1. People are more exposed to persuasive messages on a daily basis than ever before. To prove this point, simply try to recall the number of advertisements you encounter each day. Studies show that the average American is exposed to anywhere from 300 up to 3,000 advertisements per day.

2. Persuasive communication through the form of the internet, radio, and television travels more quickly.

3. There is money to be made from the business of persuasion. Many businesses are in the market purely for persuasive purposes which include public relations firms, advertising agencies, and marketing firms.

4. Contemporary methods of persuasion are more subtle.

Attribution Theory

The attribution theory of persuasion discusses how humans attempt to describe the actions of others through situational or dispositional attribution. Situational attribution, also known as external attribution is an attempt to explain the behavior of other people in the context of their environment and surroundings. Situational attribution is particularly concerned with aspects of an individual's environment that are beyond their control. An example of situational attribution would be explaining that a person's behavior is due to the home environment where he grew up rather than pointing out that it is merely his choice of actions.

On the other hand, dispositional attribution or internal attribution attempts to explain a person's behavior by looking at their individual traits, dispositions, motives, and abilities. It occurs when people do certain things because it is what is more convenient for them rather than doing what is right for those around them.

Fundamental attribution is when people incorrectly attribute an accomplishment or a shortcoming based on various external and internal factors but the opposite is true. By default humans tend to make dispositional attributions when trying to make sense out of a person's behavior when they in fact should be making situational attributions. This is especially true when we don't know a person very well therefore we don't have enough information on their situation.

When humans attempt to persuade other people to do things for us or even to simply like us, it is a tendency for us to explain positive actions with dispositional attribution. However, when we try to explain our own negative behavior we tend to use situational attribution.

Conditioning Theories

Conditioning is one of the most important concepts of persuasion. The concept of conditioning is concerned with encouraging a person to do something on their own instead of giving them a direct order to do something such as the concept of obedience.

Conditioning is widely used in the advertising industry where brands try to invoke positive feelings with their brand or logo. For this reason, brands resort to commercials that encourage people to laugh, feel sentimental, or use happy music and images. Once these commercials are through they show the brand's logo in hopes of connecting the positive emotion with their product.

Conditioning is used because emotions affect how people perceive products or brands. Humans tend to make purchases because they make them feel good. The basis of emotion is an important factor in purchasing. Advertisements are repeated because they hope that by repeating the message several times, the viewer is more likely to purchase the product as a result of connecting it with a positive emotion or experience.

Cognitive Dissonance Theory

The theory of cognitive dissonance was first proposed by Leon Festinger in 1956. According to this theory, humans naturally always strive for mental consistency. All our thoughts, attitudes and beliefs may be unrelated, in agreement, or disagreement with each other. Similarly, our thoughts, attitudes and beliefs may also be unrelated to our behavior. When we feel that there is inconsistency in our thoughts and actions it makes us feel uncomfortable. A good example of cognitive dissonance is a person who practices an unhealthy lifestyle, knowing that it is bad for him.

According to Festinger, humans feel motivated to reduce the dissonance until we feel harmony among our thoughts as well as behaviors. He suggests that there are 4 ways that humans attempt to decrease the dissonance:

1. Decrease the importance of the cognition

2. Change our minds about one or a few aspects of the behavior

3. Re-evaluate the ratio of cost/reward

4. Increase the overlap between the thought and the behavior

In the situation of the person who lives an unhealthy lifestyle, he can either make changes to adjust it and become healthier, decreases the importance of a healthy lifestyle, convince himself that he doesn't suffer a risk, or conclude that the reward of living a healthier lifestyle outweighs the benefits of living an unhealthy one.

Social Judgement Theory

Social judgement theory suggests that the natural reaction of people when presented with a persuasive idea is to seek a way to sort the information in their mind. The information is first evaluated and compared to the current beliefs held by the person also known as the anchor point or initial latitude.

These latitudes have varying levels: we tend to evaluate if it falls within the latitude of non-commitment, acceptance, rejection, or indifference. The involvement of one's ego plays a big role in determining which latitude the idea falls under. If the idea we are trying to be persuaded with is involved with how we see ourselves or anything that we care about, the latitude of non-commitment and acceptance will usually be much smaller while the latitude of rejection would then be smaller. The anchor point is a person's center of acceptance and this is when a person takes a stand when it is most acceptable to him.

When presented with information, an audience tends to first distort the information so that it fits with their own unique latitudes. When it falls within a person's latitude of acceptance, they will then integrate the information and will most likely consider it to be nearer his anchor point despite the fact that it can still be quite distant. Therefore when you are trying to persuade someone, it is important to learn about the various latitudes of your audience. The best way to succeed would be to use persuasive information which is near the latitude of acceptance for your audience if you wish to change their anchor point. When suggesting an idea repeatedly, people tend to gradually adjust their anchor points. But if you suggest ideas that fall in the rejection latitude as well as their non-commitment attitude this will not result in a change of actions or beliefs.

Inoculation theory

Inoculation theory is often observed in comparative types of adverts. The theory of inoculation suggests that one party has a weak argument whose credibility can be crushed by the audience so that they will instead go with the better argument from another party.

Narrative transportation theory

The narrative transportation theory claims that the attitudes of people can change when they lose themselves in a story. It attempts to explain the persuasive effect of stories on individuals because they may experience the narrative transportation when various preconditions are met. Furthermore, narrative transportation occurs when the listener feels like they are entering another world because the narrative evokes certain feelings especially empathy for the story's characters.

Methods of Persuasion

There are many different methods of persuasion, which are also referred to as persuasion strategies or persuasion tactics.

1. The usage of force is concerned with making demands. It can be perceived as a threat because the persuader does not give options and the audience has no choice but to follow instructions.

2. Robert Cialdini proposed 6 weapons of influence which are also used in persuasion. These are:

a. Reciprocity: Cialdini's principle of reciprocity states that when a person gives us something, we are naturally inclined to return the favor. The act of reciprocation invokes a sense of obligation in people which is often considered powerful in persuasion. The principle of reciprocity is also powerful because people feel obliged to do something in return. Humans have a natural tendency to dislike people who fail to return a favor or offer payment when given something for free. This is why reciprocation is a widely used societal standard for many cultures around the world.

b. Commitment and consistency: Consistency is deemed as one of the most important aspects of persuasion. It is a highly valued virtue in many cultures, it results in a healthy approach towards life, and offers people a shortcut in the complication of modern life.

When we experience consistency it becomes easier for us to process information and make educated decisions. People tend to commit to their actions more when they state it orally or through writing. This is why written commitments are widely used; not only do they serve as hard evidence but ideas that committed to in writing appear more psychologically concrete.

Commitment is a powerful tool in persuasion because when you are able to convince someone to commit to something they are more likely to persuade themselves and end up supplying themselves and others with reasons to support their action.

c. Social proof: By nature we are easily influenced by other people around us. It is natural for us to want to do what everyone else is doing. Oftentimes, people base their beliefs on what they see occurring in their environment. In this light, the "power of the crowd" is effective because we always want to know what other people around us are doing. Most people, without knowing, are so obsessed with what others are doing and how they act. However, social proof is only powerful when people are unsure of themselves or there are likenesses within a situation. People are more likely to conform to what other people are doing when the situation is ambiguous since there are many possibilities that can occur. Also, we are more prone to changing when people in our environment are similar to us.

d. Liking: The concept of this weapon of influence is simple: people say yes to people that they like. There are two factors that affect the likeability of an individual. The first states that physical attractiveness plays a role because people who are more attractive to other people can easily persuade others. When other people find you physically attractive it is easier to get them to do what you want. The second factor of liking is similarity, where if people like you they are more likely to say yes to what you want. It comes more naturally to people to change their opinions and beliefs for people whom they like, in fact we don't usually think about it as it happens more naturally.

e. Authority: People are more prone to listening to someone when they believe that they are an expert on a topic. When we find someone to be knowledgeable and trustworthy, we tend to listen to them more. It will be easier to persuade people when they think that you are both of these characteristics, as you already have half of the work done for you.

f. Scarcity: The concept of scarcity in persuasion is often underrated but it states that when a product is limited in availability the more valuable it becomes. Cialdini says that people want more of what they cannot have. However, when using scarcity in persuasion it is important to remember the context. Scarcity is only effective in certain contexts. If you want people to believe that a product is scarce, it needs to be clear to them what this product has that others do not.

3. Machiavellianism: This refers to the use of deceit and manipulation in order to gain power.

Aristotle also described three ways to change the mind of a person:

1. Ethos: refers to trust and how much integrity is perceived of the speaker. He must have a reputation of good character in order for him to be trusted. It is made up of 3 other elements:

a. Reputation: A person's reputation depends on their past as well as what other people say about them. In order for one to leverage reputation in order to persuade, it would entail highlighting an illustrious past and reminding other people of your achievements and successes.

b. Character: According to Aristotle, the character aspect of ethos envisions people as three-dimensional and subject to the same flaws as everyone else. People are subject to the same kinds of problems of other people. It shows a person of virtue and one who will stand by their good values.

c. Credibility: This depends on one's expertise and how it is portrayed. But for people to believe you, you must first show that you believe in yourself. You must also position yourself as an expert on the topic you wish to persuade people about. When you talk, show that you can tackle any argument thrown your way. There are also things that you can do to position yourself as a leader when you talk, such as using eye contact and hand gestures.

2. Pathos: Pathos appeals to the emotions of a person where the main goal is to arouse their interest or excitement. One of the most effective ways of arousing a person's emotions is by appealing to their values. Ethos is how people can show their values such as discussing stories where innocent people were harmed. It is a way for you to show other people what is important to them and that you put other people before you. Another way is by working with the goals of the listener, or challenging their beliefs. This is where the importance of language comes into play, because the right words can have a significant effect on people's emotions.

3. Logos: Focuses on rational explanation and cool logic together with evidence. Empirical evidence is a form of logos, necessary for

scientific proof. Providing evidence makes it difficult to deny, and it can come in the form of statistics, experience, and photographs. First-hand experience is a powerful form of evidence. Reason is another form of logos that utilizes rational points such as theories and accepted truths. If evidence does not exist, an efficient persuader can still make use of reason to prove his point. An effective way of using reasoning is by combining cause and effect.

Chapter 6: Social Impact Theory

Social impact theory was proposed by Bibb Latane in 1981. It refers to the 3 rules that define how persons can become targets of social influence. In a nutshell, social impact is the result of 3 social forces: source of impact, immediacy of the event, and the number of sources that are exerting the impact. It also states that the more targets an impact has, the smaller the impact of each individual target.

Social impact theory also utilizes mathematical equations as a way of predicting the degree of social impact in certain social situations. Latane describes social impact as the manner in which people affect others in social situations. It is observed in experiences that evoke feelings of embarrassment, humor, and persuasion among others that arise from the behavior of other people.

Latane proposed that social impact is governed by 3 laws which are translated into mathematical equations.

1. Social forces: The first rule, social forces, states that social impact occurs when a social structure is combined with social forces. The formula for this interaction is $I = f(SIN)$ whereas S is strength, I is immediacy, and N refers to the number of people.

2. Psychosocial law: States that the most significant social impact will occur from 0 to 1 sources and when the number of sources increase, the more the level of difference will even out. The equation for psychosocial law is $I = sN^t$, where power (t) of the amount of people (N) is multiplied by a scaling constant (s) whose result will determine the overall social impact.

3. Multiplication and division of impact: States that the number of targets, immediacy, and strength has an effect on social impact. In short,

the more immediacy and strength and the larger the number of targets in a social situation will result in a division of social impact on its overall targets. The equation for this law is $I = f(1/SIN)$. Social impact theory is both a specific theory as well as a generalizable theory. While it uses mathematical equations, these are also applicable to a variety of social situations. However it must be remembered that while social impact theory can explore social situations and help forecast outcomes, it also leaves some questions unanswered.

Dynamic social impact theory was developed in 1996 by Latane and his colleagues. It is considered an extension of social impact theory as it utilizes its basic principles. The primary claim of dynamic social impact theory is that social influence is greatly determined by number of sources, immediacy, and strength, as a method of explaining how both majority and minority groups influence each other.

Dynamic social theory suggests that groups of people are actually complex systems which are never static because they are always changing. Groups tend to reorganize themselves in 4 patterns:

1. Consolidation: When people engage with each other, their actions and attitudes will eventually become the same. This is why the opinions of the majority will eventually be adopted by the minority whose size will eventually decrease.
2. Clustering: People tend to gravitate towards other people who share the same opinions. Clustering is also observed when people communicate more often with those who are in closer physical proximity to them and less frequently to those who are distant.
3. Correlation: In a group, the individuals may eventually develop ideas and form the same opinions on a variety of topics even if these topics have not been discussed by the group.
4. Continuing diversity: Diversity can still exist within a group when the minority members

cluster together or majority members remain resistant with influence. Diversity is reduced when minority members are physically separated from one another, or if the majority is too large.

Chapter 7: Reverse Psychology

Reverse psychology is a technique of persuasion where a speaker utilizes a behavior that is opposite to the change he wants to occur. It is practiced with the expectation that doing so will encourage the subject to do what they desire and this is the opposite of what is actually being suggested. Reverse psychology relies on the reactance phenomenon, as discussed earlier, as it states that when there is a negative connotation to the action being persuaded, they will end up choosing the action which is forbidden.

Reverse psychology is most effective on people who are resistant. Agreeable people will go along with ideas that are being proposed to them, so these are not the audiences you should be using reverse psychology on. However, because people dislike the feeling of being manipulated, they will resist if they find out that you are using reverse psychology on them. Reverse psychology should be used subtlety on people who are resistant to direct commands.

For example, instead of telling someone: "I think it's best that you go with option x", in reverse psychology you would tell them that "It doesn't matter to me if you go with option x or y", as a way of making them think. What would follow then ideally, is for the person to go with your suggestion on their own.

Reverse psychology is often used with children because they are more vulnerable to reactance whenever there is a perceived threat to their freedom. It is a widely used practice in parenting, such as telling your children that you prefer they stay indoors when the actual desired outcome is for your children to go out and play.

In business, reverse psychology can also be very useful especially if you are in sales. However, remember not to use this technique on your superiors, it is only something that you should use on your customers. The idea here is to ignite interest in your customers by making them think that they really need your service and that their lives will not be complete without it. Used right, this technique can also lead your customers to believe that you have more to lose than they do. They may feel that you are doing them a favor and in effect they will be more eager to try your product.

Chapter 8: Practical Application of Social Influence

In Business
Social influence is crucial for a manager to be effective. It is also an important part of working in any organization, big or small. Organization members depend on each other to confirm their thoughts about and views of the world. Additionally, they will seek out and maintain norms about what they perceive to be correct or incorrect. They also influence each other to cater to the group interests.

Persuasion is particularly handy for salespeople. Customers don't like to feel like they are being sold to. However, persuasion can be useful in many facets of business. Here, we'll take a look at the characteristics of successful persuasive people:

1. Real persuasive people are purposeful. While they understand how much power they have, they don't abuse it. Instead, they use it sparingly knowing when to apply it and when not to. They know that conversations don't necessarily always require trying to convince someone to do something. Nobody likes aggressive salesmen and for this reason, successful persuaders are usually the ones that rarely ask for something. They know how to choose their battles, and when they do, they are persistent.

2. Successful persuaders are good listeners. In order for you to know how to persuade, you must also know how to listen. Pushing an argument blindly without listening to your subject may result in a futile effort. Oftentimes, being in a

persuasive mode means being a listener because by listening you will know how receptive the subject is to your idea. Listening will also give you a clue to the objections of your audience because ultimately it will be you who will have to defend this argument. It would be impossible to persuade effectively if you cannot fully understand the other person's argument.

3. Persuasive people can create an emotional connection with their audience. If someone is trying to sell you something and you have no emotional connection with them, it's easy to dismiss their ideas. This is why cold-calling clients fails most of the time. People desire to have a bond with others, without which they won't change their belief or shell out their hard-earned money on your product. Do this by showing empathy, forging a bond, and investing time in getting to know your subject or customers better. When people are aligned with your desires, it will be easier for you to persuade them.

4. Persuasive people acknowledge credibility, even those of others. They understand that everyone is entitled to their own opinions and know that the world does not function in black and white. They will show this by respecting your arguments especially in all areas where it is valid, because they know to give credit where credit is due. When you are working to persuade someone, it is important for you to acknowledge the facts that they have mentioned and reinforce it. You will be amazed at how much respect your subjects will have for you, showing you equal respect and eventually being more open when you acknowledge their opinions.

5. Smart persuaders know when it is time to be quiet. You don't win by constantly repeating a message verbally to people because it will only wear them down. Each argument should be carefully supported, and they follow through with questions that will help them understand where the subject is at. They know when to step back, and also know when to follow up.

During presentations

Speeches are powerful ways of persuading people. When done right, you can influence the entire audience's point of view on a subject even if it means strengthening an existing point of view or encouraging them to change their opinion completely.

1. Feel free to use your hands naturally when making gestures during presentations. Studies show that presenters are viewed as more competent and effective when they make hand gestures as compared to those who keep their hands still. In particular there is a connection with the way your palms are used. When speaking with your palms up it will make you seem more persuasive as well as likeable. However if you speak with your palms down, there is a greater chance that you will be perceived as more threatening or controlling.

2. When creating presentations, be selective about the words that you choose to use. It is recommended to choose words that have an

emotional impact on the audience. Words that invoke an emotion will stick with the audience longer rather than when you choose to use neutral words. Research shows that the most influential words used in presentations are: You, Because, Free, and Instantly.

3. Use the power of the 5 senses. You might be surprised at how effective engaging the other senses may be during a presentation. For example if you are experiencing technical difficulties and the projector is having some issues, play some happy or relaxing music to distract your audience as you sort out the issues. This is the same reason why companies often play relaxing music if they have to keep the customer on hold for some time.

4. When trying to persuade an audience during a presentation, using stories rather than logical arguments have been proven to be more effective. The most successful presentations in history are made up of more stories than logical arguments. It will also make people perceive you

as more credible with the ideas you are presenting. The best kinds of stories to use are those that involve suspense, metaphors and other literary techniques, and using good imagery.

5. Ask your audience to imagine doing the task you are trying to convince them to do. When the audience imagines an experience they are more likely to own the experience. The human brain cannot tell the difference between imagining reality with the actual experience.

Additionally, Aristotle's Ethos, Logos, and Pathos can also be applied to successful presentations. Here's how:

Ethos – the speaker's persona or reputation, showing the audience that you know what you are talking about.

- It is necessary to convey to your audience that you know the product or idea you are discussing. You would be hard-pressed to sell people a product that you don't know anything about. Showing your expertise also means that you have considered all possible arguments about the topic and are prepared to argue about each point when challenged.

- As a speaker, you should fully understand the audience that you are speaking to. Knowing background information on your audience will allow you to tailor messages so that it resonates with them better.

- It also helps to cite credible sources. If you are trying to sell a dental product and you are not a dentist or doctor, it will help your cause to cite a known dentist. Audiences may be forgiving even if you are not an expert in your field but it would not be an excuse not to have an expert's take on the matter. Researching what authorities in the field have to say will greatly help you in backing up your claims.

Logos – logical appeal

- In order to use logos effectively in an argument, it means more than simply referring to a fact or a number. You should also have factual information which will serve as a foundation to your argument.
- Using logos also entails "if" "then" arguments by comparing facts or events to the current situation in order to prove a point.
- Logos through the use of a sound fact makes a presenter effective in persuading because it can be difficult to deny sound logic.

Pathos - emotional appeal

- You can utilize pathos successfully through the use of presentations or speeches that contain visual aids that are meant to evoke a strong emotional response in the part of the viewer. For example, if you are trying to raise funds for typhoon victims you would appeal to the heart of the audience by showing them photos of those affected and homes that were lost.

- Storytelling can also achieve an emotional response from the audience. However, if the speaker is less confident, visuals may come more in handy. Storytelling coming from a Utopian perspective, such as explaining how life could be versus how it is in reality, is a powerful way of storytelling.

- You can also appeal to the audience's emotions by connecting to them on a personal level. This is also referred to as an ethical appeal. Speakers use an ethical appeal when there is a significant divide between the audience and speaker such as in financial status, age, or ethnicity. In these cases, the speaker would be effective in persuading when they address the divide in a way that they reduce the stigma and put both parties on a level playing field. If this is done effectively, it can create a connection so that the audience feels their values and beliefs are understood, resulting in an emotional engagement.

In Social Settings and Everyday Life

Each day we are faced with persuasion, whether we are aware of it or not. Companies want us to choose their product over another when we are shopping at the grocery store. A job offer may persuade us to choose them over another.

Influence is extremely powerful yet often overlooked. You have probably come across certain persons that are so successful with persuasion that you often wonder how they do it. Because it has proven useful, various techniques in persuasion have been observed which date back as far back as ancient times. The ultimate goal of persuasion is to convince another to adopt an idea and make it part of their core beliefs. Thanks to psychology, there are now proven ways of successfully persuading people and applying it to your everyday life. Given enough practice, you can start anew and begin your new life as a confident, successful persuader no matter where you go.

Here are proven methods you can use to persuade just about anyone:

- Choose whom to persuade and when to do it. All people can be persuadable with the correct timing. This is the reason why some political campaigns first focus their time and energy on a small set of voters who decide on elections.
- You have to persuade people who are interested in what you are saying. The way to do this is by learning how to converse with people on topics that matter to them, whether it's about love, health or money.
- Use reciprocity to your advantage, such as by doing favors for other

people. When the time comes that you ask for their support in a certain topic, you will be surprised how many people will back you up because of the things you have done for them in the past. This doesn't mean that you have to always go out of your way to do big things for people, but starting out with small gestures consistently will be key so that you can leverage reciprocity later on. Build a reputation of being someone who is generous and thoughtful, and you have half the work cut out for you.

- Persistence is key in persuasion. Successful persuaders know that they can keep asking for something because they understand their value. Be persistent in your message and it will pay off in time.
- Make it a habit to give compliments sincerely. People are positively affected by compliments and it has

become natural for us to trust people who invoke good feelings in us. Complimenting people may be one of the easiest ways you can learn how to be an effective persuader and it won't cost you anything but a few moments of sharing a good statement about someone else.

- Smart persuaders know how to manage the expectations of other people. Salesmen who promise a 20% increase in sales and come back with more than that are rewarded accordingly. Persuasion also has a lot to do with understanding expectations and over-delivering each time.
- Create a sense of scarcity. When discussing a topic or service to other people, you can be an ambassador for it when you know how to emphasize its scarcity. Sometimes the product that you want to appear scarce can even be your presence. It is all about creating

worth for a product that is not always easily available.

- Good persuaders know how to create a sense of urgency. If you want people to act on a belief right away, you'll have to emphasize the urgency and know what makes them tick.
- Effective persuaders know that images are key. This also refers to having the right first impression in all that you do, because people know that what they see is more potent than what they hear about. If you are trying to drive home a point, learn how to tell a story such that you are able to paint an image in the listener's mind of something that is desirable to them that you have the ability to provide.
- One of the most surprising practices of effective persuaders is their ability to tell the truth. They know how to tell people things about them that no one else has the guts to say. The ability to

allow other people to confront meaningful events or truths about themselves may result in surprising effects, and particularly this would be getting another person to trust you more.

- Hardly anything is more attractive than a person who is confident. As discussed earlier, humans are naturally drawn to people whom they find attractive. Regardless of whether you are in a social or business setting, confidence will go a long way in persuasion. If you believe in what you do, it will show in the way you talk about certain things.
- Timing is an important aspect of successful persuasion. You should get to know the person whom you are persuading. For example if you are trying to persuade a friend to do something, you know that weekends are the most ideal time to discuss with

them because they may be swamped with work during the week. This way they will be more receptive to your ideas.

- Repeating what people say during conversations shows that you are truly listening to them. You can prove this by saying "If I am correct, you intend to travel to Mexico on July and will be spending a total of 3 weeks there." Not everyone cares much about details but when you show that you do, you will easily make yourself likeable.

- If you are the type of person who resorts to verbal fillers, practice your speeches at home. Verbal fillers such as "ah" and "um" is the fastest way to throw your credibility out the window.

- Learn how to speak the language of the person you are talking to. Never resort to finishing another person's sentences, or interrupting them. It is considered rude and will make them feel invaded. Instead, listen closely to how other people talk and if they can't find the words, give them time. Mirror their method of communication: if they stray from jargon, do the same.

- The medium of your pitch is just as important as the message. While some people prefer to run through facts over an email, others prefer a phone call, and others prefer a direct meeting. Get to know the person you are pitching to so that you know which medium is most effective. Remember, when choosing a medium, this should be something that is about them, and not you. Your efforts in persuasion will be futile if they are not comfortable with the medium and the environment it was delivered in.
- Using future tense in conversations is a great way to display confidence. Talking in future tense also tells the other person that you are ready to

carry out the promises you've mentioned. This can easily be done by using the word "will", such as "We will do this" and "You will see this". However, it's easy to get carried away resulting in overwhelming the subject. Don't make decisions for the other person, the goal here is to start discussing possibilities and the effects of decisions that you can make together.

- People who display behavioral flexibility have more control. Showing people how flexible you are in various situations will make you likeable by the majority and eventually give you the upper hand in persuasion. One perfect example of this is the child versus the parent. In order for a child to get what they want they resort to a number of bargaining tactics that include crying, pouting, charming, and

pleading. While the parent only has a single response which is "no".
- Don't assume things without having the proper evidence to back up your claims. Instead, always offer what you can bring to the table. In business settings, we tend to assume that people find the product too expensive or don't have the money to pay for it. In reality, people are willing to spend but it is up to us to create the need and leave the choice up to them.
- Learn to be a source of good energy. You have probably heard of the term "emotional vampire", people who drain others of their own energy. If you want to be a good persuader, you should be someone who invigorates and motivates other people. You can learn how to do this by making people laugh, getting them excited, being a source of happiness, even if it's as simple as being a good listener.

In Relationships

Believe it or not, there are also principles of persuasion that can actually help you build better relationships.

- Reciprocity: When you give yourself or help another selflessly especially in times that they are experiencing distress, that person is likely to return the favor. They will be drawn to you because they will not forget being helped when they needed it the most. If you are trying to win the heart of someone, you can spark interest by doing them a favor.

    Reciprocity also entails doing something first that makes the opposite sex feel compelled to return. This could be as simple as smiling first when you encounter them, or being the first to flirt. If they are interested this can encourage them to act out on their impulses. And because you evoked positive feelings by smiling, your chances of persuading them into a date will be even better.

- Commitment and consistency: People are generally attracted to those who are consistent in their behavior. Consistency is a highly valued trait especially in relationships. If you can show a potential lover early on that you are committed to them and consistent in your actions then you have a greater chance of persuading them. It will communicate to them that investing time in you will not be a futile effort.

In the early stages of a relationship it is particularly important to show consistency. If you ask a woman out, be sure to stick with the plans. It may even take a lot of guts for a woman to agree to a date with you, so don't ruin her trust by changing the plans. Showing her that you can be relied on no matter what will make her feel good about investing time in you.

- Social proof: This principle states that people are more inclined to base their actions on what those around them are doing. In the world of relationships, this translates to desiring a man who has a thriving social group or dating a woman whom your friends like. Here are other ways to make social proof work for you in relationships:
    - Build genuine friendships with women who have boyfriends. By going out as a group this may lead you to meet their single friends, who will almost automatically like you because you have one foot in the door already: approval from a good friend.
    - Socialize with female friends and their boyfriends too. When women

see that others are enjoying your company, you will be perceived as desirable. They will assume that if their friends like you, you are good company.
- o Make friends with staff of restaurants and bars that you frequent. Doing so shows that you have real social status and are of value to other people. It shows that you are popular and in-demand, piquing the curiosity of dates who will want to get to know you better.
- o If you want to go the distance in demonstrating social value, host a party. This will show your date that you are an admired and well-liked person.

- Liking: People are easily influenced by people that they like. Certain factors come into play here, such as physical attractiveness, people who compliment us, and people who make us laugh. Here are some tips to apply this principle in the dating scene:

- Both men and women should always look tidy and keep facial hair in check. Eyebrows should be clean, beards should be trimmed.
- Invest in dressing well especially when you are going out to meet new people. It is human nature to treat others better when they look good. You only have a few minutes to make a good impression on the member of the opposite sex and if you dress sloppily, you've wasted a chance.
- Show a positive attitude – people are inclined to spend time with other people when they exude happiness, joy, and warmth. Nobody likes to hang out with people who complain a lot, this

kind of behavior is a major turn off in societies. Learn how to feel good about yourself, laugh a lot, and make other people feel good – this is a surefire way to make people feel good about being around you.

- Authority: People feel more obliged to listen to people who evoke a sense of authority. In dating and relationships, it is still possible to demonstrate authority even if you aren't necessarily in a position of power. For example, a man who shows he is in full control of his destiny and emotions is perceived as attractive. Showing authority over yourself is attractive to the opposite sex.

One of the key methods in demonstrating authority is by speaking in a dominant tone. Think about how prominent public figures always speak with a sense of authority and confidence. On the contrary, talking with a meek tone suggests that you have no authority and are not in control. It also shows in the way you speak; inviting someone for a drink using "Come grab a drink with me" shows more authority rather than asking permission: "Would you like to have a drink with me?"

Authority can also be showed in these ways:

- Be more assertive especially when it comes to discussing what you need and want. Don't be ashamed to go after your goals. If someone begins to cross your boundaries, speak up about it.
- Body language can say more about authority than you think. Hold your head high and keep your back straight. Look people in the eye when you are engaging in conversation with them.

- Scarcity: People are more attracted to others when their availability is limited. In the dating world, this means that the more available you are, the less desirable you are. Similarly, when information is limited, people want that information more. However, this should not be mistaken with playing hard to get. Don't fake being too busy to make time for someone you are trying to impress or persuade to go on a date with you. Instead, work on creating a fulfilling lifestyle because you have so many other things to do. When the opposite sex sees that you are content with the activities you have on your plate, they will know the time they spend with you is truly valuable.

Conclusion

Understanding the psychological aspects of persuasion is a very useful tool in everyday life. As you have read, there are many ways of understanding each facet of persuasion as well as the different forms of persuasion. When you understand how to effectively persuade people, you can enjoy the benefit of improved relationships at work, in your personal life, and in social settings because you will learn how to manipulate situations and people to act in your favor without them realizing it. You'll be able to manipulate people into doing almost anything you want, eventually making you more successful. Persuasion is a powerful, valuable skill that can take you further in life.

Other books available by author on Kindle, paperback and audio

Unbreakable Willpower: Learn The Amazing Secrets Of Self Control Self Discipline And The Art Of Mental Training

Made in the USA
Lexington, KY
07 July 2015